Ancient History Advent Calendar

24 Days with 180+ Captivating Facts about Ancient History and Civilizations for young and old

TABLE OF CONTENTS

TEST YOUR KNOWLEDGE WITH OUR QUIZ APP!

Every day, you will learn many exciting facts about Ancient history in this book. To test your knowledge, we have prepared some exciting quiz questions!

You can scan the QR code below, enter your email address, and you will receive free access to the Quizlet mobile app.

There you will find four quiz questions for each day that are related to the exciting facts in this book!

In the Quizlet app, you can click on the "Learn" function, which will bring up multiple-choice questions where you can test your knowledge.

SCAN THE QR CODE AND GET FREE ACCESS:

https://livetolearn.lpages.co/ancient-history-advent-calendar/

Quizlet is completely free for you. The app has a paid version, but you don't need it.

DOOR 1

THE FIRST CITIES AND WRITING

The very first cities weren't big or had tall buildings like the ones we see today. Instead, they were busy towns made of mudbrick houses. These ancient cities were built in a region called Mesopotamia. That name means "land between the rivers" in ancient Greek. The people who lived there were called the Sumerians. They gathered together for safety and to work on big projects.

THE FIRST HOMEWORK

Imagine a school day over 5,000 years ago! Students in ancient Mesopotamia learned to write on clay tablets using a system called cuneiform. This wasn't easy! Scribes used a reed stylus to press wedge-shaped marks into the wet clay. If a student made a mistake, they couldn't just erase it—they had to smooth out the clay and start all over again. Sometimes, a teacher would punish a student for bad handwriting, proving that a love-hate relationship with homework has existed for a very, very long time.

A Story for the Ages

The very first stories ever written down were on clay tablets. One of the most famous is the *Epic of Gilgamesh*, a tale about a powerful king who goes on an adventure to find the secret to living forever. The story is full of monsters, gods, and a great flood. For thousands of years, people told this story, and then it was lost to time. But in the 1800s, archaeologists found the ancient clay tablets, and this amazing adventure story was brought back to life!

A Secret Language

In Sumer, only a small number of people, called scribes, knew how to read and write cuneiform. This was a very valuable skill. Scribes were some of the most important people in society, second only to the kings and priests. They were the record keepers, poets, and storytellers of their time. They had a job that most people couldn't even dream of doing. This made them super important and probably a little bit snobby, too.

ANCIENT INVENTIONS FROM MESOPOTAMIA

The Wheel: The first wheels weren't for cars. They were used by potters to make clay vessels! This simple invention changed how people moved and traded forever.

The Sail: To travel faster on rivers, the Mesopotamians invented the sail. This made it easier to trade goods and travel long distances without having to row their boats.

The Plow: Farmers needed a way to prepare their fields for planting. The plow, which was pulled by oxen, made farming much faster and more efficient.

Brewing Beer: Yes, you read that right! The very first recipe ever found was for beer. It was a thick and lumpy drink, but people loved it.

The First Written Laws: The world's first known code of laws was written in Mesopotamia by a king named Ur-Nammu. This was a list of rules and punishments to help keep everyone in line.

Door 2

The Akkadian Empire

THE WORLD'S FIRST EMPIRE

The Akkadian Empire was the very first empire in the history of the world! It was founded by a powerful king named Sargon the Great. He conquered and united all the warring city-states of Mesopotamia. Before the Akkadians, each city was its own nation. Under Sargon's rule, they became part of a massive empire.

FROM GARDENER TO KING

The story of King Sargon is amazing. According to legend, he started life as a simple gardener. He then became a cupbearer for a king and eventually became a legendary military leader. His incredible rise to power shows that anyone, no matter their start, can achieve great things. Sargon's legacy lasted long after his death. He became a hero for later Mesopotamian kings.

THE FIRST OFFICIAL LANGUAGE

The Akkadians had their own language called Akkadian, which they used for everything from government laws to business records. Akkadian became the official language of the empire. It was used to communicate across a huge territory. It was written using a system of wedge-shaped marks on clay tablets, a type of writing that the Akkadians borrowed from the Sumerians.

THE STELE OF A GOD-KING

One of the most famous pieces of Akkadian art is the Victory Stele of Naram-Sin, a stone carving that shows one of the Akkadian kings as a powerful god-like figure. In the artwork, the king is shown stepping on his enemies. He wears a horned helmet to show that he is divine. This artwork is a symbol of the empire's power and its proud leaders.

Building the First Empire

First Postal System: The Akkadians might have created the world's first postal system. They used clay tablets and envelopes to send letters to different parts of the empire.

New Gods: The Akkadians adopted many of the Sumerian gods, but they also added their own, like the goddess of war and love, Ishtar.

Controlled Trade: They controlled major trade routes that stretched all the way from the Persian Gulf to the Mediterranean Sea. Trade made them very wealthy.

First Dynasty: The family of King Sargon ruled the empire for over 150 years. This made them the first royal family in history to lead an empire.

DOOR 3

THE INDUS VALLEY CIVILIZATION

A Language We Can't Read

The Indus Valley civilization is one of the biggest mysteries of the ancient world. They had a complex system of writing, but we still have no idea what it says! No one has ever been able to figure out what their script means. It's like a secret code that has never been broken. Because we can't read their records, we have a lot of unanswered questions about their history and daily life.

The First Planners

The cities of the Indus Valley were incredibly well planned. They were built on a grid system with straight streets that crossed each other at perfect right angles. The houses were made of standardized mudbricks. Homes even had private bathrooms that connected to an underground sewer system! This shows that the people were very organized and cared a lot about being clean.

THE GREAT BATH

One of the most impressive discoveries in the Indus Valley city of Mohenjo-daro was the Great Bath. It was a large public pool that was probably used for religious rituals or community gatherings. Its existence shows that the people of this civilization cared about public spaces and possibly had some kind of ritual for cleanliness. It was like a very, very old community pool!

NO KINGS, NO PALACES?

Unlike other great civilizations like Egypt and Mesopotamia, we haven't found any evidence of huge palaces or statues of kings in the Indus Valley. This has led many historians to believe that they were a peaceful society without a single, all-powerful ruler. It's possible that the cities were led by a group of merchants or priests who worked together instead of having a king.

Amazing Creations from the Indus People

Standardized Weights: They used a uniform system of weights and measures for trade. This shows that they were organized merchants and that trade was very important to them.

First to Wear Cotton: The Indus Valley people were among the first in the world to grow cotton. They made it into clothing.

Intricate Seals: They created beautiful, small stone seals. These seals had carvings of animals and their mysterious script. They were likely used to mark goods for trade.

Ancient Toys: Archaeologists have found many toys, including small clay animal figures and even dice. They likely enjoyed playing games.

DOOR 4

LIFE IN ANCIENT EGYPT

THE RIVER OF LIFE

Step out of the desert and into the fertile land of ancient Egypt. The most important part of the ancient Egyptians' world was the Nile River. It was their everything! The Nile gave them water to drink, rich soil for farming, and a super-convenient highway for travel. Without the Nile's predictable floods, which brought fresh, fertile mud to the fields every year, ancient Egypt would not have existed.

MAKEUP FOR A PURPOSE

Both ancient Egyptian men and women wore makeup, but it wasn't just to look good. They used a dark black eyeliner called kohl to draw lines around their eyes. This helped to protect their eyes from the harsh desert sun and to keep flies away. Scientists now know that the kohl they used also helped to prevent eye infections. It was a very smart invention!

THE FIRST DOCTORS

Ancient Egyptian doctors were ahead of their time. They were experts at setting broken bones and had an amazing understanding of the human body. They even used moldy bread on wounds to help them heal. We now know that some molds contain a form of penicillin, so this strange-sounding remedy was actually a very clever and effective way to fight off infections.

THE FIRST CALENDAR

The ancient Egyptians were very good at keeping track of time. Their entire calendar was based on the predictable rhythm of the Nile River's floods. They divided their year into three seasons: inundation (when the river flooded), growth (when they planted their crops), and harvest (when they gathered their crops). This system was essential for their survival and planning, and it was a simple but effective way to organize their year.

THE DAILY DIET OF THE EGYPTIANS

Bread and Beer: Bread and beer were the two most important foods. They were a part of almost everyone's meals.

Healthy Vegetables: They ate lots of vegetables, especially onions, garlic, and lettuce. They grew these veggies in the rich soil along the Nile.

Dates as Dessert: Dates were a favorite. They were sweet and easy to store and transport.

Fish and Fowl: For protein, they ate fish from the Nile River. They also caught ducks and geese.

Sweet Honey: Honey was their main sweetener. They didn't have sugar. They used it to sweeten desserts and drinks.

DOOR 5

THE PHARAOHS AND PYRAMIDS

THE TALLEST BUILDING

The Great Pyramid of Giza is one of the most incredible buildings ever made. For almost four thousand years, it was the tallest manmade structure in the world! It was built as a tomb for a pharaoh named Khufu. It's a huge mystery how the ancient Egyptians were able to build such a massive and precise structure without any modern technology.

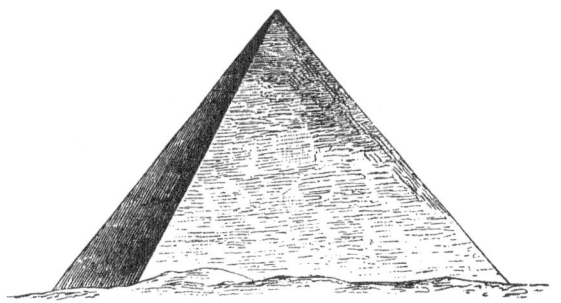

THE CAT LOVERS

The ancient Egyptians loved cats so much that they considered them sacred animals. Cats were a big part of their lives. They were more than just pets. Cats protected the home from pests like snakes and mice. If you killed a cat, even by accident, the punishment was death! The ancient Egyptians even mummified their cats and buried them with a lot of care. This shows just how much they were loved and revered.

JOURNEY TO THE AFTERLIFE

Ancient Egyptians believed in an afterlife and thought they could take their things with them. This is why pharaohs were buried with so many treasures, furniture, and food. To get to this afterlife, their bodies had to be preserved through a process called mummification. This complicated process took seventy days! It involved a lot of salt and bandages.

MORE THAN A KING

Pharaohs were much more than just rulers. They were considered living gods on Earth. The pharaoh was the leader of the army, the head of the government, and the most important religious figure. They had a huge amount of power. Everything they said was considered law. People treated them with a lot of respect since they believed the pharaoh was the link between the gods and the people.

What a Pharaoh Took with Them

Jewelry and Gold: To show their power and wealth in the next life.

Furniture and Tools: So they could have a comfortable home in the afterlife.

Food and Wine: To eat and drink on their journey.

Statues of Servants: To serve them in the afterlife.

Sacred Scrolls and Amulets: To protect them on their journey to the underworld.

Door 6

The Kingdom of Kush

A Rival to Egypt

The Kingdom of Kush was an ancient civilization located in a region of Africa called Nubia, which is in modern-day Sudan. Most people have heard of ancient Egypt, but not as many know about the Kingdom of Kush. It was a strong and powerful kingdom in Africa that sometimes fought with Egypt. Kush even ruled over it at times! The Kushites had their own unique culture, religion, and way of life.

More Pyramids than Egypt

The ancient Kushites built their own pyramids. They actually built more of them than the ancient Egyptians did! The Kushite pyramids were different, though. They were smaller, much steeper, and often had a small temple built at the front. Over 200 of these pyramids can still be seen in Sudan today. They stand as a reminder of their long history.

Warrior Queens

Unlike many other ancient civilizations, the Kingdom of Kush was often ruled by powerful queens called kandakes. These queens led their armies into battle and were a key part of Kushite society. The kandakes are a great example of powerful female leadership in the ancient world.

Rich in Gold

The Kingdom of Kush was incredibly wealthy, mainly because of its large supply of gold. The name Nubia actually comes from the ancient Egyptian word for gold. This great wealth allowed the Kushites to build magnificent temples and palaces. It also gave them the power to be a major trading partner with other civilizations, including Egypt and Rome.

Kush's Place in History

Conquered Egypt: For about 100 years, the Kushites ruled over Egypt. They formed Egypt's Twenty-fifth Dynasty.

Their Own Alphabet: The Kushites had their own alphabet called Meroitic. It has still not been fully deciphered by historians.

Lion God: The most important Kushite god was the lion god Apedemak. He was the god of war and was often shown with a human body and a lion's head.

Iron Production: The Kushites were experts at working with iron. They were one of the first in Africa to develop iron production on a large scale.

Door 7

The Minoans

A Civilization on an Island

The Minoan civilization was an ancient culture that lived on the island of Crete, in the middle of the Mediterranean Sea. Because they were surrounded by water, they became master shipbuilders and sailors. Their powerful ships allowed them to trade with other civilizations all over the ancient world. They were one of the first great European civilizations. They were known for their huge and beautiful palaces.

The Unwalled City

One of the most surprising things about the Minoan civilization is that its palaces and cities often did not have walls! In a time when most civilizations built massive walls to protect themselves, the Minoans seemed to have nothing to fear. Many historians believe they were protected by their powerful navy, which was so strong that no one dared to attack them on their island.

The Minotaur's Maze

The most famous Minoan palace was the Palace of Knossos (/ˈnɒsəs/), which was so big and complex that it likely inspired the famous Greek myth of the Minotaur. According to the myth, the Minotaur was a monster that lived in a maze under the palace. It would eat anyone who couldn't find their way out. The maze of rooms, staircases, and corridors in the palace probably made people feel like they were in a real labyrinth (a complex maze)!

The Dangerous Sport

Minoan artists loved to paint pictures of a very dangerous and exciting sport called bull leaping. A person would grab the horns of a charging bull and then flip over its back to land on their feet on the other side. This acrobatic feat was likely part of a religious ceremony. These paintings show how important bulls were to their culture. It must have taken a lot of bravery to perform this stunt!

Interesting Facts about the Minoans

No King? Some historians believe that Minoan society might have been run by women. It's unclear if they had a king, but women seemed to have a lot of power and respect.

Lost Writing: The Minoans had a writing system called Linear A, but no one has been able to read it yet! It's one of ancient history's greatest mysteries.

Volcanic Eruption: Many historians believe a powerful volcanic eruption on a nearby island caused huge tidal waves and ash clouds. These might have helped to destroy their civilization.

Skilled Traders: The Minoans traded with civilizations as far away as Egypt. They exchanged olive oil, wine, and pottery for gold, jewels, and other valuable goods.

Door 8

The Phoenicians

Master Sailors and Traders

The Phoenicians (/fəˈnɪʃəns/) were an ancient people who lived along the coast of the eastern Mediterranean Sea. They were master sailors and traders who built an amazing civilization on the water. Their ships traveled to every corner of the Mediterranean, from ancient Greece to Spain. They created a vast network of trade routes, carrying valuable goods from one civilization to another. They spread their culture far and wide.

The World's First Alphabet

The Phoenicians are most famous for inventing the world's first true alphabet! Unlike the complicated hieroglyphs of the Egyptians, the Phoenician alphabet had only 22 simple letters. Each letter represented a single sound, making it much easier to learn and use. This clever system of writing was eventually adopted and adapted by the Greeks and Romans. It is the ancestor of the alphabet we use today.

The Color of Kings

The Phoenicians were known for a special purple dye they made. It was called Tyrian purple. This dye was made from thousands of tiny sea snails. These snails were difficult to get, which made the dye very expensive. Because of its rarity, only kings and very rich people could afford to wear clothes colored with the dye. This made Tyrian purple a famous symbol of royalty and power throughout the ancient world.

Pioneers of Glass

The Phoenicians were amazing craftspeople and pioneers in glass-making. They discovered how to create beautiful glass objects, like jewelry and small perfume bottles. They perfected the technique of blowing glass. These intricate and colorful glass items were highly valued. They became a major part of their trade with other civilizations. The Phoenicians were the first artists of glass.

Phoenician Facts You Might Not Know

The City of Carthage: The Phoenicians founded the city of Carthage in North Africa. It became a powerful trading city that was a rival to ancient Rome for centuries.

Not One Kingdom: The Phoenicians were not a single unified empire. Instead, they were a group of independent city-states that each had its own ruler.

Valuable Murex Snails: It took thousands of tiny *Murex* snails to make just a small amount of their famous purple dye. This is why it was so expensive!

Trade Everywhere: The Phoenicians were so successful at trading that they established colonies and trading posts all over the Mediterranean coast.

Door 9

The Ancient Greeks

The Home of Democracy

The ancient Greeks gave us a revolutionary idea called democracy, which means "rule by the people." Instead of being ruled by a king, the citizens of Athens could vote on laws and decisions that affected their city. However, only men who owned property were considered "citizens," so it wasn't a perfect system. But it was a huge first step toward the kind of government many countries have today, where people get to have a say in how they are governed.

The First Olympics

Did you know that the Olympic Games started in ancient Greece? They were a series of athletic competitions held every four years in honor of the god Zeus. Athletes from all the Greek city-states came together to compete in sports like running, wrestling, and chariot racing. The games were so important that all conflicts stopped during the event. This was known as the Olympic Truce.

THE GREAT THINKERS

Ancient Greece was home to some of the most brilliant minds in history, like Socrates, Plato, and Aristotle. These philosophers were not just sitting around thinking about the meaning of life. They were asking big questions about science, politics, and how the world worked. Their ideas shaped Western thought for thousands of years and are still studied by students and scholars today.

THE BIRTH OF DRAMA

The ancient Greeks loved going to the theater. They were the ones who invented modern drama. They had plays that were funny (comedy) or sad (tragedy). These plays weren't just for entertainment, though. They were often about politics, religion, and morality. They taught people important lessons about life. Their theaters were huge outdoor arenas built into hillsides. They had incredible acoustics. This means sound carried really well. Everyone could hear the actors speak.

Cool Facts about Greek Mythology

Twelve Olympians: There were twelve main gods and goddesses who lived on Mount Olympus. Zeus and Hera were two of the most important.

Monsters and Heroes: Their myths were full of wild monsters like the Minotaur and heroic figures like Hercules.

Tricky Gods: The gods weren't always nice. They often played tricks on humans and each other.

The Trojan Horse: One of the most famous stories is about the Trojan War, which was won by hiding soldiers inside a giant wooden horse.

Daily Life: The Greeks believed that gods were involved in every part of their lives, from farming to war.

Door 10

The Spartans

Tough from the Start

Welcome to Sparta, a city-state where life was all about being a tough warrior. The first rule started right at birth! A newborn baby was inspected by a council of elders. If the baby was deemed weak or unhealthy, it was considered a burden to the city. The baby would be abandoned on a mountainside. This might sound incredibly harsh, but the Spartans believed it was the only way to make sure their society was strong.

The Ultimate Boot Camp

At the age of seven, Spartan boys were taken from their homes and began their military training in a brutal program called the agoge. They were taught to fight, hunt, and endure extreme pain. They slept on uncomfortable reeds, were given very little to eat, and were encouraged to steal food to survive. The idea was to make them disciplined and resourceful soldiers who could withstand anything.

A Wall of Shields

The most famous Spartan warriors were the hoplites. They were known for their large, round shield called the hoplon (/'hɒp.lɒn/). They fought in a tight, disciplined formation called a phalanx (/'fæl.æŋks/). The phalanx was a terrifying wall of men and shields. Each soldier's shield protected the man next to him. This formation was nearly unbeatable, and it made the Spartan army the most feared fighting force in all of Greece.

Strong Women, Strong Sons

Unlike other Greek city-states, where women stayed in the home, Spartan women were given more freedom. They were encouraged to be strong and healthy by training in athletics and gymnastics. The Spartans believed that strong mothers would have strong babies who would grow up to be great warriors. This focus on physical fitness gave Spartan women a level of respect and independence that was rare in the ancient world.

The Rules of Spartan Life

The Red Cloak: Spartan soldiers wore red cloaks. It's believed the color helped hide their blood, making it harder for enemies to know they were injured.

Black Broth: The most famous Spartan meal was "black broth," a horrible stew of boiled pork, blood, and vinegar. It was so bad that it was a test of bravery just to eat it.

Iron Money: Spartans used heavy iron bars as money. This made it difficult to gain wealth. It kept the Spartans focused on simple living instead of getting used to luxury.

No Leaving Town: Spartans were restricted from traveling. This was to prevent them from bringing back foreign ideas that could change or corrupt their traditional warrior culture.

DOOR 11

THE PERSIAN EMPIRE

A Giant Empire

The Persian Empire was one of the biggest empires the world had ever seen. At its peak, it stretched from the border of India all the way to Greece and Egypt. This massive empire was founded by Cyrus the Great. It grew to include over twenty million people. To govern such a huge area, the Persians divided their land into different provinces, each with its own ruler. All of them were loyal to the Persian king. This system kept the vast empire organized and running smoothly.

The Royal Road

The Persians were masters of organization. They built an incredible highway system called the Royal Road. This road was over 1,600 miles long and had regular stations with fresh horses. It worked so well that a message could travel from one end of the empire to the other in just seven days! This allowed the king to send orders and receive news very quickly, which helped him to keep control over his enormous kingdom.

THE KING OF KINGS

The ruler of the Persian Empire was known as the King of Kings. This title showed just how powerful he was. The kings lived in incredible palaces, like the one in Persepolis, which had magnificent columns and carvings. The king was seen as sacred. No one was allowed to approach the king without his permission. He was the most powerful person in the empire, and his word was law for millions of people.

ZOROASTRIANISM: THE FIRST MONOTHEISTS?

The main religion of the Persian Empire was Zoroastrianism. It is one of the world's oldest monotheistic religions (religions that believe in only one god). It was founded by the prophet Zoroaster and centered on the belief in one god, Ahura Mazda, who represented truth and light. Followers believed in a constant battle between good and evil. They thought humans had to choose which side to be on. It is still practiced by a small number of people today.

Persian Life and Innovations

The World's First Refrigerator: The Persians invented the yakhchal (/jæk'tʃæl/), a clever, dome-shaped building. It was used to store ice and keep food cold for a long time, even in the hot desert sun.

A New Way to Drink: The Persians developed a unique water management system called qanat (/qəˈnɑːt/). These were underground tunnels that moved fresh water from the mountains to cities and villages without it evaporating.

The First Human Rights Declaration: Cyrus the Great is famous for creating the Cyrus Cylinder. This clay cylinder is considered the first declaration of human rights. It freed some slaves and promoted religious freedom.

DOOR 12

ALEXANDER THE GREAT

TAUGHT BY A GENIUS

As a teenager, Alexander had an amazing teacher: the famous philosopher Aristotle. For three years, Aristotle taught Alexander about science, medicine, philosophy, and Greek literature. Alexander took these lessons to heart. He grew up with a deep appreciation for Greek culture. This is a big reason why he would later spread Greek ideas and learning throughout the lands he conquered.

THE BOY KING

Alexander the Great was a Macedonian king who conquered a massive empire in just ten years. He did it all before he turned thirty-three! He led his army across Greece, into Egypt, and all the way to India. He never lost a battle, and his military tactics are still studied by generals today. Ancient tales say his ambition was so great that he cried when he ran out of new lands to conquer.

THE GORDIAN KNOT

There was a legend that whoever could untie a complex knot called the Gordian Knot would become the ruler of Asia. Many people tried and failed. When Alexander arrived, he didn't bother trying to untie it. Instead, he simply drew his sword and sliced the knot in half! This showed everyone that Alexander was a man who solved problems in his own way. It also proved that he was destined to be a great ruler.

A CITY BY ANY OTHER NAME

Alexander founded over twenty cities. In a move that showed he was a bit full of himself, he named almost all of them Alexandria. The most famous of these cities is Alexandria in Egypt. It became a center of learning, trade, and culture. It was home to a massive library that held scrolls from all over the world.

Alexander's Amazing Legacy

A New Era: His conquests led to the Hellenistic Age, a period when Greek culture and ideas spread from Greece to India. These ideas blended with local traditions to create a new way of life.

Born a King: Alexander became the king of Macedon at the young age of twenty after his father was killed. Alexander immediately set out to take over the world.

A Famous Horse: His horse's name was Bucephalus (/bjuːˈsɛfələs/), and he rode it into many of his battles. Alexander even named a city after his horse.

Military Genius: Alexander is considered one of the greatest military generals in all of history. He never lost a single battle, despite leading his army against massive empires.

DOOR 13

THE FOUNDING OF ROME

Raised by a Wolf

According to an ancient legend, the city of Rome was founded by twin brothers, Romulus and Remus. The two were abandoned as babies. They were miraculously found and raised by a she-wolf! Later, they decided to build a city on the spot where they were found. They had a huge argument about who would be the king. In a fit of rage, Romulus killed his brother and named the city after himself. What a dramatic way to start a city!

A Master of Copying

The Romans were very good at borrowing ideas from other cultures. They saw the amazing gods and goddesses of the ancient Greeks and simply adopted them for their own religion, although they gave them different names. For example, the powerful Greek god Zeus became the Roman god Jupiter. The goddess Hera became Juno. The Romans believed it was smart to use good ideas, no matter where they came from.

The Army that Conquered

The Roman army was known for being one of the most powerful fighting forces in the ancient world. Their soldiers were very well trained and disciplined. They fought in massive groups called legions. A legion was made up of thousands of soldiers. Their organization, fighting tactics, and engineering skills allowed them to conquer a huge empire that lasted for hundreds of years.

A Triumphant Parade

A Roman general who won a big victory was celebrated with a huge parade called a triumph. The general would dress like a god and ride through the city in a fancy chariot. His soldiers would march behind him. The people he had captured in battle would be paraded through the streets as well. It was the highest honor a general could receive, and it was a way for all of Rome to celebrate a great victory.

Latin Words We Still Use

Agenda: The word agenda comes from Latin and means "things to be done." You probably have something on your to-do list right now!

A.M. & P.M.: These abbreviations stand for ante meridiem (/ˌænti məˈrɪdiəm/), meaning "before noon," and post meridiem, which means "after noon." They help us tell time.

Etc.: This common abbreviation comes from the Latin phrase et cetera, which means "and other things."

Veni, Vidi, Vici: Julius Caesar famously said this after a quick victory. It means, "I came, I saw, I conquered."

DOOR 14

ROMAN DAILY LIFE

LAUNDRY WITH A STINK

Ancient Romans had a strange way of doing laundry. They used public urinals to collect urine, which was used as a key ingredient for washing clothes! The ammonia in urine is a powerful cleaning agent. The Romans used urine to get tough stains out and make their togas a bright white. So, next time you see a laundromat, be glad you live in a world with soap and washing machines!

DINNER PARTIES ON COUCHES

If you were a rich Roman, your dinner parties were called convivia (/kɒnˈvɪviə/). Guests would recline on special couches called triclinia (/trɪˈklɪniə/) while being served food and wine. They would talk and gossip for hours. The food could be very exotic, like cooked flamingo tongues or stuffed dormice. These parties weren't just for eating, though. They were also a way to show off your wealth and social status.

The Secret to Rome's Power

The Romans were incredible builders. They had a secret weapon: concrete! They were the first to widely use a version of concrete, which was so strong that many of their buildings, like the Pantheon, are still standing today. The Romans used concrete to build massive monuments, huge public buildings, and the aqueducts that brought water to their cities.

Socializing at the Spa

For ancient Romans, going to the public baths was a huge part of daily life. The baths, called thermae (/ˈθɜːrmeɪ/), were like a gym, a spa, and a shopping mall all rolled into one. People would go there to bathe, exercise, read books in the library, and catch up on the latest gossip. It was a place for everyone, from the rich to the poor, to relax and socialize.

Inventions from the Roman World

Paved Roads: The Romans built a massive network of paved roads that connected their entire empire. These roads were made so well that some are still in use today!

Aqueducts: They invented the aqueduct, a system of channels and bridges that carried fresh water from the mountains to the cities.

Central Heating: The Romans invented the hypocaust (/ˈhaɪ.pə.kɔːst/), a system of underfloor heating that kept their homes and bathhouses warm in the winter.

The Julian Calendar: Julius Caesar introduced a calendar that is the direct ancestor of our modern one. It had 365 days and a leap year every four years.

DOOR 15

THE ROMAN COLOSSEUM AND GLADIATORS

Entertainment on a Grand Scale

The Colosseum in Rome was a massive amphitheater. It was built to hold over fifty thousand spectators. It was used for all sorts of public entertainment. Imagine a stadium so big that the entire population of a large town could fit inside! The Romans loved their spectacles, and the Colosseum was the ultimate venue for them. The people could see everything from dramatic battles to exotic animals.

Fighters for Fame

Gladiators were professional fighters who battled each other or wild animals for the entertainment of the crowds. Most gladiators were slaves, prisoners of war, or criminals. Some free men chose to become gladiators for the fame and fortune it could bring. They trained hard and developed different fighting styles. Gladiators were often huge celebrities in their day. The roar of the crowd must have been deafening during their fights!

MOCK SEA BATTLES

Believe it or not, the Romans sometimes flooded the Colosseum to stage mock sea battles called naumachiae (/nɔːmɑːˈkiː/). They would bring in real ships and have them fight it out in the filled arena. This incredible feat of engineering showed off the Romans' ability to stage truly spectacular events. It must have been an amazing sight to see warships battling in the middle of the city!

THUMBS UP OR DOWN?

You've probably seen movies or shows where the emperor gives a "thumbs up" or a "thumbs down" to decide if a defeated gladiator would live or die. While this image is popular, historians aren't sure if it's accurate. What we do know is that the crowd played a big role in the decision. They would shout their opinions. A well-fought battle could earn a gladiator rest from fighting. Sometimes, they could even win their freedom after years of fighting.

SPECTACLES OF ANCIENT ROME

Chariot Races: Held in massive stadiums like the Circus Maximus, chariot races were very popular and dangerous. Teams would wear different colors and race around an oval track. There were often crashes and spills.

Theater Performances: Roman theaters staged plays that ranged from comedies to tragedies. Actors wore large masks to portray different characters. These dramatic performances were an important part of Roman culture.

Public Executions: Public executions were also a form of entertainment. Criminals would be put to death in gruesome ways for the amusement of the crowds.

Animal Hunts: The Romans often staged hunts called venationes (/vɛnəˈtɪəniːz/). Exotic animals from across the empire would be brought to the arena to fight each other or be hunted by trained men.

DOOR 16

ROMAN EMPERORS

The First Emperor

The Roman Republic ended when a man named Augustus took control. He became the first Roman emperor. He was a brilliant leader who wasn't a cruel tyrant like some of the emperors who came after him. He brought an era of peace and stability to the Roman Empire that lasted for over two hundred years. This period was known as the Pax Romana, or "Roman Peace."

The Emperor and His Horse

One of the most famous Roman emperors was Caligula. He was strange and unpredictable. He once tried to make his favorite horse a Roman consul! A consul was one of the highest government officials. While it's not clear if he was serious or just making a joke, it shows just how strange some of the Roman rulers could be.

A Split Empire

The Roman Empire became so big that it was eventually split into two parts to make it easier to rule. The Western Roman Empire, which included Rome itself, eventually collapsed. The Eastern Roman Empire, also known as the Byzantine Empire, survived for almost another thousand years! It continued to use Roman laws and traditions. The Eastern Roman Empire was a powerful force in the world long after Rome had fallen.

Not an Emperor, but a Dictator

When we think of a Roman ruler, we often think of Julius Caesar. Did you know that he was never actually an emperor? He was a powerful general and dictator. He was so popular that the members of the Senate—a group of important men who made laws for Rome—feared he would become a king and destroy the Roman Republic. Some of the senators killed him, but his death actually led to the end of the Roman Republic and the rise of the Roman Empire.

Five Famous Roman Emperors

Augustus: The first Roman emperor who brought a long period of peace to the empire.

Nero: An emperor known for his cruelty and for supposedly playing the lyre—a stringed instrument—while Rome burned.

Caligula: A very strange emperor who was famous for his wild and unpredictable behavior.

Trajan: The emperor under whose rule the Roman Empire reached its largest size, stretching from Britain to the Middle East.

Hadrian: An emperor who traveled a lot and was known for building a massive wall in Britain to protect the northern border of the empire.

DOOR 17

ANCIENT INDIA

A King with a Change of Heart

The Mauryan Empire was one of the largest and most powerful empires in ancient India. It was ruled by a fearsome king named Ashoka. He was known for his brutal conquests. However, after winning a war where he saw hundreds of thousands of people killed, he was so filled with regret that he had a complete change of heart. He gave up violence and became a peaceful follower of Buddhism.

The Great Pillar of Ashoka

After his conversion to Buddhism, Emperor Ashoka wanted to share his message of peace and kindness with all his people. He had new rules and teachings carved into huge stone pillars and rocks across his massive empire. The Pillars of Ashoka are some of the oldest examples of Indian art and writing. They are a symbol of his transformation from a warrior king to a peaceful ruler.

Medicine Ahead of its Time

Ancient Indian medicine was incredibly advanced for its time. Doctors understood many parts of the human body and knew how to perform complex surgeries. They used a wide variety of herbs and plants as medicines. They even had instruments for surgery that look a lot like the ones doctors use today. They wrote down their medical knowledge on scrolls, which helped to pass it on to future generations.

A Message of Peace

Ashoka's change of heart had a huge impact on the empire. He banned the killing of animals for sport and food. He built hospitals and rest houses for both people and animals. Ashoka also sent Buddhist missionaries to spread his message of peace to other countries, including Sri Lanka and the Middle East. His peaceful rule helped to make Buddhism a major world religion.

World-Changing Indian Innovations

The Concept of Zero: Ancient Indian mathematicians were the first to use the concept of zero as a number. This was a huge step for mathematics. The number zero is very important for calculations today.

Buttons: Buttons were invented in the Indus Valley. At first, they were used just for decoration, but they later became a part of clothing.

The Game of Chess: The game of chess originated in ancient India. It was called chaturanga (/tʃætʊˈræŋgə/). It was a strategy game used to teach military tactics.

The Ruler: A very early form of the ruler was invented in the Indus Valley. It was a simple tool used to measure things. Rulers are still used by students and engineers everywhere.

DOOR 18

THE FIRST DYNASTIES

THE STORY OF DYNASTIES

The history of ancient China is a long and rich story. It is often told in a series of dynasties. A dynasty is a family that rules a country for a long period of time. It passes power from one generation to the next. The Shang dynasty was one of the very first to leave behind a lot of archaeological and written records. They were a powerful family, and their way of ruling would shape China for thousands of years.

ASKING THE GODS

During the Shang dynasty, kings asked for advice from their gods and ancestors using oracle bones. A question would be carefully carved into a flat piece of animal bone or a turtle shell. The bone would then be heated until it cracked. A priest would interpret the pattern of the cracks to get an answer from the gods. This was a form of ancient fortune-telling. The writings on these bones are also the earliest known examples of Chinese script.

The Mandate of Heaven

The Zhou dynasty, which followed the Shang, created a powerful idea to justify their rule: the Mandate of Heaven. This concept said that the king's power came directly from the gods. As long as the ruler was just and fair, the gods would allow him to rule. However, if he became cruel or lazy, the gods would take their mandate away and give it to a new family. This new family could then rightfully overthrow the old dynasty and begin a new dynasty.

Not a Single Wall

The Great Wall of China is one of the most famous structures in the world, but it was not originally built as one single wall. For centuries, different dynasties built walls to protect their lands from invaders from the north. These walls were later connected and expanded by powerful emperors like those from the Qin and Han dynasties. They turned it into the massive, winding structure we know today.

China's World-Changing Inventions

Gunpowder: This powerful explosive was invented by ancient Chinese alchemists who were trying to find a recipe for a medicine that would make people live forever.

Paper: An official from the Han dynasty named Cai Lun is credited with inventing paper in 105 CE. Paper made it easier to write and record information.

The Compass: The magnetic compass was invented in ancient China for fortune-telling. It was later used for navigation, helping sailors find their way across the oceans.

Silk: The secret of making silk was kept by the Chinese for thousands of years. This luxurious fabric became the most valuable item traded on the Silk Road.

DOOR 19

ANCIENT JAPAN

THE GODS OF NATURE

One of the oldest religions in Japan is Shinto, which means "the way of the gods." Shinto focuses on the worship of kami (/ˈkɑːmi/), which are spirits or gods that live in nature. A kami can be in a waterfall, a mountain, or even a rock! Shinto teaches people to deeply respect nature. It is a core part of Japanese culture. Shinto shrines can be found in some of the most beautiful natural places.

AN UNBROKEN LINE

The Japanese imperial family is the world's oldest royal family. The current emperor can trace his family line back over 2,600 years! In ancient Japan, the emperor was considered to be a living god. The ruler was descended from the sun goddess Amaterasu. While the emperor is not seen as a living god today, the emperor is still a very important symbol of Japan's history and culture.

THE WAY OF THE WARRIOR

Ancient Japan was ruled by a class of highly skilled warriors called the samurai. They lived by a strict code of honor known as Bushido, which means "the way of the warrior." This code taught them to be brave, loyal, and disciplined, even in the face of death. Samurai fought with their famous katana swords. They were expected to protect their lord and their honor at all costs.

A CLOSED-OFF COUNTRY

For over two hundred years, Japan was almost completely closed off from the rest of the world. This period was called Sakoku (/ˈsɑːkoʊku/), or "locked country." The Japanese government banned almost all foreign visitors and prevented the Japanese people from leaving the country. This isolation allowed Japanese culture to develop and flourish on its own without outside influences. It was a unique and fascinating chapter in their history.

Traditions of Ancient Japan

Kanji Characters: The Japanese writing system uses characters called kanji. They were borrowed and adapted from China.

The Art of Paper: After paper was introduced from China, the Japanese turned it into an art form called origami. This involved carefully folding paper into unique shapes.

Tea Ceremony: The tea ceremony is a beautiful and peaceful ritual of preparing and serving tea. It is a very important part of Japanese culture and tradition.

Cherry Blossoms: The gorgeous cherry blossoms, or sakura, are a symbol of the beautiful but fleeting nature of life. It is a key theme in Japanese thought.

DOOR 20

THE BABYLONIAN EMPIRE

THE GATE OF THE GODS

Step into the city of Babylon, a place so grand its name meant "the Gate of the Gods." This ancient city was a marvel of engineering. The city was surrounded by massive walls that were said to be so wide that two chariots could drive side by side without bumping into each other! The city was a bustling center of trade and culture. Its walls were a symbol of its power and wealth. Babylon was one of the most famous cities of the ancient world.

THE FIRST JUSTICE SYSTEM

If you think your parents have a lot of rules, you should have met King Hammurabi! He was the king of Babylon. He created one of the first sets of written laws. It was known as the Code of Hammurabi. These laws were carved onto a giant stone pillar called a stele. That way, everyone could see them. Some of the laws were pretty harsh, like the famous "eye for an eye" rule. If you hurt someone, you could expect to be hurt in the same way.

Stargazing Superstars

The Babylonians were known for looking at the stars. They were some of the first people to create detailed maps of the night sky. They could even predict when eclipses would happen. Their knowledge of astronomy was so advanced that they named many of the constellations we still use today, like Leo and Scorpio. They believed that the stars could tell them about the future, which is why they were some of the first astrologers.

An Ancient Mystery

One of the most talked-about places in Babylon was the Hanging Gardens. They were one of the Seven Wonders of the Ancient World. The gardens were said to be a beautiful terraced paradise, with plants and trees growing high in the air. The problem? We don't know for sure if they ever really existed! No one has ever found any solid proof. The Hanging Gardens remain one of the biggest mysteries of the ancient world.

What Did Babylonians Eat?

So Much Barley: They ate a lot of barley, which they made into bread and porridge. This was their main food source.

Sweet Dates: Dates from palm trees were a major part of their diet. Dates were sweet and easy to grow.

Sesame Seeds: They used sesame seeds to make oil and as a spice for their food.

Hearty Stews: They loved to cook stews and roasts in clay ovens, much like we do today.

Beer with a Straw: The Babylonians loved to drink beer, but it was so thick and chunky that they had to use a straw to drink it.

DOOR 21

THE ANCIENT OLMECS

A "MOTHER CULTURE"

The Olmecs were the first great civilization in ancient Mesoamerica, which is the region that includes modern-day Mexico. Because they were the first, many historians call them the "mother culture." They laid the groundwork for later civilizations like the Maya and the Aztecs. Their ideas about religion, art, and even games were passed down for hundreds of years.

HEADS OF STONE

The Olmecs are most famous for their massive stone heads. These colossal heads are sculptures of human faces carved from a single piece of volcanic rock. Some of the heads are as tall as a bus and weigh over 40 tons! It's believed they are portraits of powerful Olmec rulers, but no one knows for sure. How they moved these huge stones without metal tools is a mystery.

THE FIRST TO PLAY BALL

The Olmecs are credited with inventing the first version of the famous Mesoamerican ball game. The game was played with a heavy rubber ball and was a mixture of sport and religious ritual. Later, the Maya and Aztecs adopted and changed the game, but it all started with the Olmecs. They were the first to play with a rubber ball.

A MYSTERIOUS VANISHING ACT

The Olmec civilization was a powerful and advanced society, but around 400 BCE, it mysteriously disappeared. Their cities were abandoned, and their way of life ended. Historians aren't sure exactly why, but they have a few ideas. It could have been because of climate change or volcanic eruptions that ruined their crops. Maybe they were conquered by another group. The answer is lost to history.

THE OLMECS' FIRSTS

A Compass: The Olmecs might have been the first to use a compass. Archaeologists found a polished magnetic stone that points north.

The Number Zero: The Olmecs are credited with inventing the concept of the number zero. This was an important step for mathematics and astronomy in the Americas.

Complex Calendars: They developed complex calendars based on their knowledge of the stars and planets. This discovery was later used by the Maya.

Rubber: The Olmecs were among the first to use rubber. They made the heavy balls for their ball game from the sap of rubber trees.

DOOR 22

THE ANCIENT MAYA

A Civilization of City-States

The ancient Maya were not a single unified empire like the Romans or Persians. Instead, they were a group of independent city-states. These city-states were like small countries. They had their own kings, armies, and pyramids. However, they all shared a common culture, religion, and writing system. These things united them.

Masters of Time

The Maya were brilliant astronomers and mathematicians. They created a highly accurate and complex calendar system. They had two main calendars that worked together: a 365-day solar calendar for farming and a 260-day sacred calendar for religious events. Their calendars were so precise that they could predict eclipses and other celestial events.

A Deadly Ball Game

One of the most popular pastimes for the Maya was a game called pitz. Two teams would try to hit a heavy rubber ball through a high stone hoop using only their hips, elbows, and knees. This game had deep religious meaning. Sometimes, the losing team captain—or even the winning team captain—would be sacrificed to the gods!

The First Chocoholics

The Maya were among the very first people to discover and enjoy chocolate! They made a bitter, foamy drink out of cacao beans. They often spiced it with chili peppers. This chocolate drink was so special that it was used in ceremonies and religious rituals. It was mostly enjoyed by kings and nobles. This ancient drink is a far cry from the sweet chocolate bars we eat today, though!

Maya Achievements and Innovations

Rubber: The Maya were among the first to create rubber from the sap of trees. They used it to make the heavy balls for their famous ball game.

Writing System: They developed the most advanced writing system in all of ancient America. They used a series of hieroglyphs—pictures that represent words or sounds—to record their history and beliefs.

Mathematics: The Maya invented a complex number system that included the concept of zero.

Observatories: They built massive stone structures that served as observatories. Priests and scholars used them to study the stars and planets.

DOOR 23

THE ANCIENT AZTECS

A City on a Lake

The Aztec capital city, Tenochtitlan (/tɛˌnɒtʃtɪˈtlɑːn/), was built on an island in the middle of a huge lake. It was a truly remarkable city. It had a population of over 200,000 people at its peak! To get around, the Aztecs built long land bridges called causeways. They connected the island to the mainland. The city was a maze of canals and floating gardens. It was a unique and powerful center for their empire.

Floating Gardens

To feed their massive city, the Aztecs had to get creative. They built chinampas (/tʃɪˈnæmpəs/), which were floating gardens made by weaving together reeds and mud from the bottom of the lake. They would plant crops on these floating rafts, which gave them a lot of land to grow food. This amazing invention was a smart way to turn a huge lake into a food source.

A Bloody Belief

The Aztecs believed that the sun was a god that needed human blood to keep it strong and to make it rise every day. To please their gods, they performed human sacrifices on a large scale. They built massive temples, like the Templo Mayor in Tenochtitlan, where these rituals took place. While it seems gruesome to us, the Aztecs believed it was necessary to keep the world from ending.

Popcorn and Chocolate

The Aztecs were among the first people to enjoy popcorn and chocolate. They ate popcorn as a snack, but they also used it as a decoration for their headdresses and statues of gods. They drank a bitter, spicy chocolate beverage. It was considered a sacred drink for warriors and nobles. It was so valuable that they even used cacao beans as a form of money!

Aztec Achievements and Inventions

First to Require School: The Aztecs were one of the first civilizations to have mandatory education for every child, regardless of whether they were rich or poor.

The Calendar Stone: The Aztec calendar was a system with two cycles. One had 260 days, and the other had 365 days. The Sun Stone showed how they used the sky to track time.

Tribute System: The Aztec Empire became rich and powerful by demanding tribute from the people it conquered. This meant the conquered cities had to pay them with goods and food.

Rubber: Like their Maya predecessors, the Aztecs learned how to make and use rubber from the sap of trees. They used this sap for their famous ball game.

DOOR 24

THE ANCIENT INCAS

A Highway in the Sky

The Inca Empire was the largest empire in the Americas. It stretched across the Andes Mountains. To connect their massive empire, the Incas built an amazing system of roads that stretched over 25,000 miles. These roads were a network of paved paths, suspension bridges, and tunnels. They linked the mountain cities to the coast. This incredible feat of engineering kept their huge empire together.

A Message in a Knot

The Incas did not have a written language like the Romans or the Egyptians. Instead, they used a system of knotted colored strings called quipu to record information. Different colors and types of knots stood for numbers, names, and even stories. Only a few people knew how to "read" the knots. The Incas used this unique system to keep track of everything from population numbers to taxes.

STONE-CUTTING MASTERS

The Incas were absolutely amazing at working with stone. They built incredible buildings and temples, like the city of Machu Picchu, without using any mortar (a paste used to hold bricks or stones together). They carefully carved huge stones so they fit together perfectly. It was like a giant puzzle. You couldn't even fit a knife blade between the stones! These walls were very strong and could survive earthquakes.

THE ORIGINAL POSTAL SERVICE

To send messages across their huge empire, the Incas used highly trained runners called chasqui (/'tʃɑːski/). The chasqui would run at top speed along the roads, carrying messages or small packages. The runners worked in relays, which means they passed the message to the next runner every few miles. This human postal service was very fast and efficient.

Incan Innovations and Culture

Potatoes: The Incas were one of the first people to cultivate potatoes. They grew thousands of different kinds of potatoes. They even developed a way to freeze-dry them for storage.

Llamas: The llama was the most important animal to the Incas. They were used for their wool, their meat, and as a way to carry goods over the mountains.

Skull Surgery: Inca doctors were skilled surgeons who were able to perform a type of skull surgery called trepanation. This helped relieve swelling in the brain.

Gold and Silver: The Incas had a lot of gold and silver, which they believed were the "sweat of the sun" and the "tears of the moon." They used these precious metals to decorate their temples.

Source reference

Chapter 1:

The Sumerians: Joshua J. Mark, "Sumer," World History Encyclopedia. Cuneiform & Gilgamesh: British Museum, "The Epic of Gilgamesh"; Joshua J. Mark, "Cuneiform," World History Encyclopedia. Mesopotamian Inventions: University of Chicago, "The Oriental Institute" (The Sumerians); Joshua J. Mark, "Ur-Nammu," World History Encyclopedia. First written laws: The Metropolitan Museum of Art (Mesopotamia: The Code of Ur-Nammu).

Chapter 2:

The Akkadian Empire: World History Encyclopedia ("Akkadian Empire"); History.com ("Sargon of Akkad"). Sargon the Great: Britannica ("Sargon of Akkad"); World History Encyclopedia ("Sargon of Akkad"). Akkadian Language & Art: World History Encyclopedia ("Akkadian Language"); The British Museum ("Akkadian Art"). Naram-Sin Stele: The Louvre Museum ("Victory Stele of Naram-Sin").

Chapter 3:

Indus Valley Civilization: World History Encyclopedia ("Indus Valley Civilization"); Britannica ("Indus Civilization"). Mohenjo-daro: World History Encyclopedia ("Mohenjo-daro"); Britannica ("Mohenjo-daro"). Indus Script: National Geographic ("The Indus Script Hasn't Been Deciphered"); The British Museum ("Indus Script Seals").

Chapter 4:

The Nile River: National Geographic Society ("The Nile River"); Smithsonian National Museum of Natural History ("Ancient Egypt"). Egyptian Makeup: World History Encyclopedia ("Ancient Egyptian Cosmetics").

Egyptian Medicine: The Metropolitan Museum of Art ("The Art of Medicine in Ancient Egypt"). Egyptian Calendar: The University of Memphis ("The Egyptian Calendar"). Egyptian Food: The British Museum ("Ancient Egyptian Food and Drink").

Chapter 5:

The Great Pyramid: National Geographic Society ("Great Pyramid of Giza"); History.com ("Pyramids in Egypt"). Egyptian Mummification: The British Museum ("Mummification"); World History Encyclopedia ("Ancient Egyptian Mummification"). Cats in Egypt: Smithsonian Magazine ("The Cult of the Cat in Ancient Egypt"); History.com ("Why Were Cats So Revered in Ancient Egypt?"). Pharaohs: The Metropolitan Museum of Art ("Egyptian Kingship").

Chapter 6:

The Kingdom of Kush: National Geographic ("Ancient Nubia"); World History Encyclopedia ("The Kingdom of Kush"). Pyramids: World History Encyclopedia ("Nubian Pyramids"); UNESCO ("The Pyramids of Kush"). Kandake: National Geographic ("The Powerful Queens of Kush"); History.com ("Kandake"). Gold and Resources: The British Museum ("Kush: The Land of Gold"); World History Encyclopedia ("Meroe").

Chapter 7:

Minoan Civilization: World History Encyclopedia ("Minoan Civilization"); Britannica ("Minoan Civilization"). Knossos Palace: History.com ("Knossos"); The Metropolitan Museum of Art ("The Minoans"). Bull Leaping: The British Museum ("Bull-Leaping Fresco"); History.com ("Bull Leaping"). Minoan Mysteries: World History Encyclopedia ("Linear A and Linear B"); National Geographic ("Santorini Volcano").

Chapter 8:

The Phoenicians: World History Encyclopedia ("The Phoenicians"); History.com ("Phoenicians"). Phoenician Alphabet: Britannica ("Phoenician Alphabet"); World History Encyclopedia ("Phoenician Alphabet"). Tyrian Purple & Glass: The Metropolitan Museum of Art ("Tyrian Purple"); World History Encyclopedia ("Phoenician Glass"). Carthage: Britannica ("Carthage"); History.com ("Carthage").

Chapter 9:

Ancient Greek Democracy: The British Museum ("Ancient Greece: Democracy"); The Metropolitan Museum of Art ("The Athenian Agora and the Democracy of Athens"). The Olympic Games: The University of Pennsylvania Museum of Archaeology and Anthropology ("The Ancient Olympic Games"); The British Museum ("Ancient Greece: The Olympics"). Greek Philosophers: The Stanford Encyclopedia of Philosophy ("Ancient Greek Philosophy"); History.com ("Ancient Greek Philosophy"). Greek Drama: The National Theatre of Greece ("Ancient Greek Theatre"); History.com ("Ancient Greek Theater").

Chapter 10:

Spartan Society: Paul Cartledge, The Spartans: An Epic History; World History Encyclopedia ("Sparta"). Military Training: History.com ("Spartan military training"); Britannica ("Sparta: The agoge"). Hoplites and Phalanx: The Metropolitan Museum of Art ("The Spartan Army"); World History Encyclopedia ("Spartan Army"). Spartan Women: Ancient History Encyclopedia ("Spartan Women").

Chapter 11:

The Persian Empire: The Metropolitan Museum of Art ("The Achaemenid Persian Empire"); World History Encyclopedia ("Cyrus the Great").

The Royal Road: The Oriental Institute of the University of Chicago ("The Royal Road"); History.com ("Ancient Persia's Royal Road"). Zoroastrianism: Britannica ("Zoroastrianism"); The British Museum ("The Cyrus Cylinder"). Persian Innovations: The Ancient History Encyclopedia ("Persian Innovations"); National Geographic Society ("Yakhchal").

Chapter 12:

Alexander's Life: Britannica ("Alexander the Great"); History.com ("Alexander the Great"). Gordian Knot: Livius.org ("The Gordian Knot"); World History Encyclopedia ("Gordian Knot"). Alexandria: History.com ("Library of Alexandria"); World History Encyclopedia ("Alexandria").

Chapter 13:

The Founding of Rome: Britannica ("Romulus and Remus"); World History Encyclopedia ("Romulus"). Roman Gods and Army: History.com ("Ancient Roman Gods"); World History Encyclopedia ("Roman Legion"). Roman Triumph: Britannica ("Roman Triumph"). Latin Phrases: Merriam-Webster Dictionary ("E.g."), Britannica ("Carpe diem"), World History Encyclopedia ("Veni, vidi, vici").

Chapter 14:

Roman Daily Life: World History Encyclopedia ("Roman Daily Life"); History.com ("Ancient Roman Daily Life"). Roman Concrete: Smithsonian Magazine ("The Secrets of Ancient Rome's Concrete"); World History Encyclopedia ("Roman Concrete"). Public Baths: Britannica ("Roman Baths"); The Roman and Greek World, PBS ("Roman Baths"). Roman Inventions: History.com ("10 Innovations That Show Roman Engineering Was Amazing"); World History Encyclopedia ("Roman Technology").

Chapter 15:

The Colosseum: Britannica ("Colosseum"); World History Encyclopedia ("Colosseum"). Gladiators: History.com ("Gladiators"); The British Museum ("Gladiators"). Naumachia: World History Encyclopedia ("Naumachia"); Princeton University ("Naumachia"). Roman Entertainment: Britannica ("Roman Games"); The Roman and Greek World, PBS ("Public Entertainment").

Chapter 16:

Augustus: Britannica ("Augustus"); World History Encyclopedia ("Augustus"). Caligula: History.com ("Caligula"); World History Encyclopedia ("Caligula"). Splitting the Empire: Britannica ("Roman Empire"); History.com ("Fall of the Roman Empire"). Julius Caesar: World History Encyclopedia ("Julius Caesar"); History.com ("Julius Caesar"). Famous Emperors: Britannica ("Roman Emperors"); World History Encyclopedia ("List of Roman Emperors").

Chapter 17:

The Mauryan Empire: Britannica ("Mauryan Empire"); World History Encyclopedia ("Mauryan Empire"). Ashoka: History.com ("Ashoka the Great"); World History Encyclopedia ("Ashoka"). Ashoka's Pillars and Edicts: Britannica ("Ashoka Pillars"); World History Encyclopedia ("Edicts of Ashoka"). Ancient Indian Medicine: World History Encyclopedia ("Ancient Indian Medicine").

Chapter 18:

Chinese Dynasties: World History Encyclopedia ("Chinese Dynasties"); Britannica ("Chinese Dynasties").

Oracle Bones: The Metropolitan Museum of Art ("Anyang and the Shang Dynasty"); World History Encyclopedia ("Oracle Bones"). Mandate of Heaven: World History Encyclopedia ("Mandate of Heaven"); History.com ("Zhou Dynasty"). The Great Wall: History.com ("The Great Wall of China"); National Geographic ("Great Wall of China"). Chinese Inventions: World History Encyclopedia ("Inventions of Ancient China"); History.com ("Ancient Chinese Inventions").

Chapter 19:

Shinto: Britannica ("Shintō"); World History Encyclopedia ("Shinto"). Japanese Emperor: National Geographic ("The Japanese Monarchy"); World History Encyclopedia ("List of Japanese Emperors"). Samurai: History.com ("Samurai"); Britannica ("Samurai"). Sakoku: World History Encyclopedia ("Sakoku"); History.com ("Why Japan Isolated Itself from the World").

Chapter 20:

King Hammurabi and the Code: The Metropolitan Museum of Art (The Code of Hammurabi); World History Encyclopedia ("Hammurabi"). Babylonian Astronomy: The British Museum ("Babylonian astronomy"); History.com ("Ancient Mesopotamia"). Hanging Gardens: National Geographic Society ("The Seven Wonders of the Ancient World"). Babylonian Food: The Oriental Institute of the University of Chicago ("Food and drink in Ancient Mesopotamia").

Chapter 21:

The Olmecs: History.com ("Olmec Civilization"); World History Encyclopedia ("Olmec Civilization"). Colossal Heads: The Metropolitan Museum of Art ("Olmec Art"); National Geographic ("Olmec Colossal Heads"). Olmec Culture: World History Encyclopedia ("Olmec Culture"); History.com ("Olmec Ballgame"). Olmec Inventions: World History Encyclopedia ("Olmec Technology"); National Geographic ("Mesoamerican Ballgame").

Chapter 22:

Maya Civilization: World History Encyclopedia ("Maya Civilization"); History.com ("Maya"). Mayan Calendars: National Geographic ("The Mayan Calendar Explained"); Britannica ("Maya Calendar"). Maya Ball Game: World History Encyclopedia ("Mesoamerican Ballgame"); History.com ("Ancient Mayan Ball Game"). Mayan Chocolate: World History Encyclopedia ("Cacao in Mesoamerica"); Smithsonian Magazine ("The Sweet Story of Chocolate").

Chapter 23:

The Aztecs: World History Encyclopedia ("Aztec Civilization"); History.com ("Aztec Empire"). Tenochtitlan & Chinampas: Britannica ("Tenochtitlan"); National Geographic ("Chinampas"). Aztec Religion & Sacrifice: History.com ("Why the Aztecs Practiced Human Sacrifice"); The Metropolitan Museum of Art ("Aztec Religion"). Aztec Innovations: World History Encyclopedia ("Aztec Technology"); History.com ("Aztec Innovations").

Chapter 24:

The Inca Empire: Britannica ("Inca"); History.com ("Inca"). Inca Roads & Quipu: UNESCO ("Qhapaq Ñan"); World History Encyclopedia ("Inca Roads"). Machu Picchu & Stone Masonry: National Geographic ("Machu Picchu"); History.com ("Machu Picchu"). Inca Innovations: World History Encyclopedia ("Inca Technology"); Smithsonian Magazine ("The Amazing Feat of Inca Surgery").

Printed in Dunstable, United Kingdom

70247886R00067